W9-BBG-714

MOON FLIGHT ATLAS

EXPLORING THE MOON

1969-1972

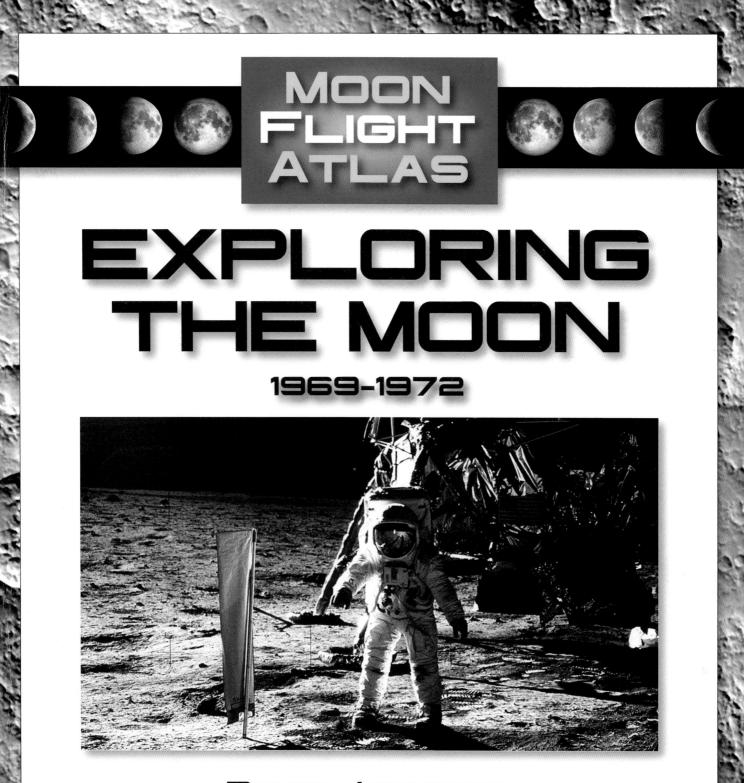

DAVID JEFFERIS

CRABTREE
PUBLISHING COMPANY
WWW.CRABTREEBOOKS.COM

INTRODUCTION

With the safe landing of **Apollo 11** in 1969, the ancient dream of travel to the Moon finally came true. When astronauts Neil Armstrong and Buzz Aldrin set down their Lunar Module, it was a time of new and exciting discoveries.

In these pages you can read about the six successful Apollo missions to the Moon—and the flight that nearly ended in disaster.

Crabtree Publishing Company

www.crabtreebooks.com   1-800-387-7650

Written and produced for Crabtree Publishing by:
David Jefferis

Technical advisor:
Mat Irvine FBIS (Fellow of the British Interplanetary Society)

Editors:
Mat Irvine, Ellen Roger

Proofreader:
Melissa Boyce

Prepress Technicians:
Mat Irvine, Ken Wright

Print Coordinator:
Katherine Berti

Acknowledgements
Acknowledgements
We wish to thank all those people who have helped to create this publication and provided images.

Individuals:
Mat Irvine
David Jefferis
Gavin Page
The Design Shop

Organizations:
NASA
Smithsonian National Air and Space Museum
The Observer, London

The right of David Jefferis to be identified as the Author of this work has been asserted by him in accordance with the Copyrights, Designs and Patents Act 1988.

Printed in the U.S.A./042019/CG20190215

Library and Archives Canada Cataloguing in Publication

Jefferis, David, author
          Exploring the moon, 1969-1972 / David Jefferis.

(Moon flight atlas)
Includes index.
Issued in print and electronic formats.
ISBN 978-0-7787-5409-1 (hardcover).--
ISBN 978-0-7787-5418-3 (softcover).--
ISBN 978-1-4271-2213-1 (HTML)

          1. Moon--Exploration--History--Juvenile literature. 2. Space flight to the moon--History--Juvenile literature. 3. Project Apollo (U.S.)--History--Juvenile literature. 4. Moon--Maps--Juvenile literature. 5. Moon Juvenile literature. I. Title.

TL799.M6J44 2019   j629.45'409   C2018-905617-7
                                                                         C2018-905618-5

Library of Congress Cataloging-in-Publication Data

Names: Jefferis, David, author.
Title: Exploring the moon : 1969-1972 / David Jefferis.
Description: New York, NY : Crabtree Publishing Company, [2019] | Series: Moon flight atlas | Includes index.
Identifiers: LCCN 2018060552 (print) | LCCN 2019001645 (ebook) | ISBN 9781427122131 (Electronic) | ISBN 9780778754091 (hardcover : alk. paper) | ISBN 9780778754183 (pbk. : alk. paper)
Subjects: LCSH: Project Apollo (U.S.)--Juvenile literature. | Space flight to the moon--Juvenile literature. | Moon--Exploration--Juvenile literature.
Classification: LCC TL789.8.U6 (ebook) | LCC TL789.8.U6 J44 2019 (print) | DDC 629.45/4--dc23
LC record available at https://lccn.loc.gov/2018060552

MOON FLIGHT ATLAS

CONTENTS

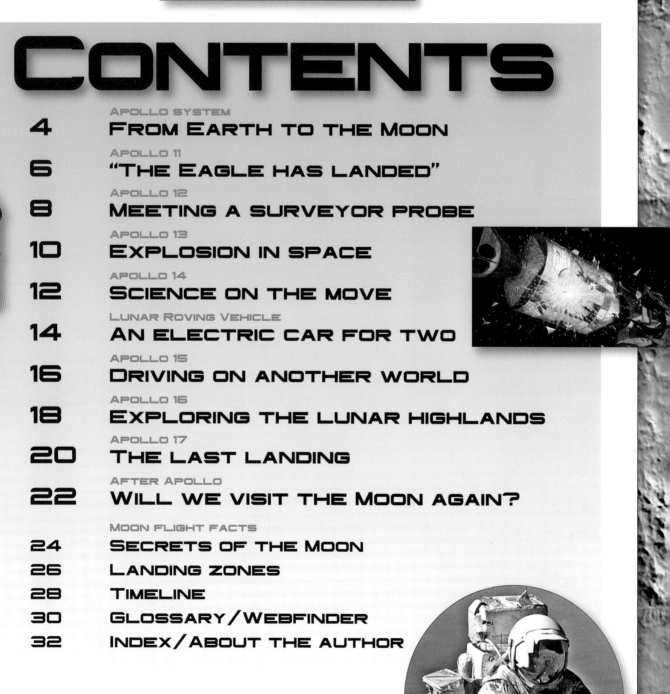

FROM EARTH TO THE MOON

Apollo Moon flights all used the same basic hardware, the first of these being the huge Saturn V rocket that was used to launch each mission from the ground.

??? How big was the Saturn V rocket?

From top to bottom, the Saturn V ("5") towered at 360 feet (110 m) high. It consisted of three main **stages**, each one dropping away when its fuel was used up. The most powerful first stage was used for lift-off. It had five engines, roaring with a combined thrust of nearly 3,858 tons (3,500 metric tons).

← The moment of lift-off for Apollo 11, the first Moon-landing mission. The "pencil" at the top was part of the launch escape system. In an emergency, rockets could pull the Command Module out of danger.

"Gee, that launch tower is just a few feet off to one side! And then when they tell you, 'Launch tower clear,' you kinda say 'Oh, whoosh, that's good, we don't have to worry about hitting that,' and off you go from there."
Michael Collins, Apollo 11 CM pilot talks about the Saturn V lift-off

??? Where did the astronauts sit?

Each Apollo mission had a crew of three astronauts. They sat in the top, cone-shaped Command Module (**CM**), which was attached to the Service Module (**SM**) behind it. The SM had a rocket motor with fuel tanks, and also supplied power for the electronic and other systems. Together, the Command and Service Modules were called the **CSM**.

??? How far is the Moon?

The Moon **orbits** Earth about 239,000 miles (385,000 km) away. It takes about a month to complete an orbit.

The trip from Earth to the Moon took the Apollo spacecraft about three days, after which the craft went into orbit around the Moon itself.

The CSM continued to circle the Moon, while the Lunar Module was flown down to the surface.

Earth

Moon

⬆ The Moon is far smaller than Earth. Even so, its land area is huge—about the same as the combined area of Africa and Australia.

Escape tower

Command Module

Service Module

Lunar Module

Third stage

Second stage

First stage

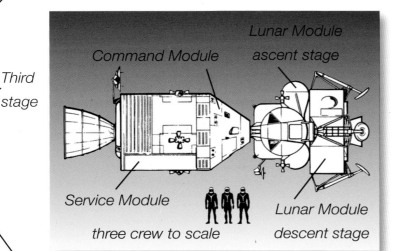

Command Module

Lunar Module ascent stage

Service Module

three crew to scale

Lunar Module descent stage

Neil Armstrong at the LM control panel

??? What about the Lunar Module?

The Lunar Module (**LM**) was a spidery machine with its own motors and air supply, and was designed to carry two astronauts to and from the Moon's surface. The third crew member stayed in the CSM, orbiting the Moon alone until it was time to link up with the returning LM. All three astronauts then returned to Earth in the CSM "mother ship."

APOLLO 11

"THE EAGLE HAS LANDED"

Neil Armstrong

Michael Collins

Buzz Aldrin

With those famous words, Neil Armstrong and Edwin "Buzz" Aldrin went down in the history books. They set down their Eagle lunar Module in the Sea of Tranquility on July 20, 1969.

➜ Collins stayed in the Command Module, high above the Moon. Armstrong and Aldrin flew down to the surface.

??? Did they land in the right place?

Not quite—in fact, their target area was covered in boulders, which could have tipped over the LM on landing. So Neil took over control, and flew the LM to a clearer spot. He made the right decision, though they had only 25 seconds of fuel left when they landed.

← Armstrong took most of the pictures, but you can see his figure and the LM here, both reflected in the visor of Aldrin's space helmet.

"The Eagle has wings!"
Neil Armstrong said this
as he examined the LM
and got ready to leave
orbit for the Moon.
Below, his famous words
when taking the first step
onto the lunar surface:
"That's one small step
for [a] man, one giant
leap for mankind."

⬆ Buzz Aldrin (in circle) as he crawled backwards out of the LM's porch. Once his feet were on the ladder, he could climb down to the surface.

??? Did astronauts weigh less on the Moon?
Yes, because the Moon has a smaller **gravity** pull than the bigger Earth, and objects weigh just one-sixth as much there. In their bulky space suits, Neil and Buzz learned to walk around easily, using a sort of "bunny hop" movement.

??? How long did they stay on the Moon?
From touchdown to takeoff, Armstrong and Aldrin were on the Moon for just over 21.5 hours. They collected soil and rock samples weighing 47.51 pounds (21.55 kg) in all.

➔ *This metal plaque was mounted on the Lunar Module's descent stage. They are both still on the Moon, more than 50 years later.*

MEETING A SURVEYOR PROBE

Apollo 12 landed on the Moon in November 1969, just four months after the triumph of Apollo 11.

??? Who flew on the Apollo 12 second Moon-landing mission?

Apollo 12 was commanded by Charles "Pete" Conrad, with Alan Bean as Lunar Module (LM) pilot. Richard Gordon stayed in lunar orbit, while Conrad and Bean left in the LM. They landed in the Ocean of Storms, named by the ancient Romans, though there are no storms there. The Moon has no oceans or atmosphere, so it has no weather.

⬆ *From left, Pete Conrad, Richard Gordon, and Alan Bean.*

??? What were the aims of the Apollo 12 mission?

The target area for Apollo 12 was the landing site of the Surveyor 3 space probe, which had landed in April 1967. Among other measurements, the probe had proved the surface could take the weight of a heavy machine.

Conrad and Bean aimed to land near the probe to see if it was still in good condition. Had the searing daytime Sun burned away its metal skin? Had freezing nights wrecked its electronics? They were about to find out!

Commander Pete Conrad nicknamed the landing zone "Pete's parking lot." The actual touchdown point was only 1,180 feet (360 m) away from Surveyor 3, which had landed two years before.

Solar panels supplied the probe with electricity from sunlight

TV camera

Pete Conrad inspects the probe. He and Alan Bean removed some parts to take back to Earth.

The LM Intrepid landed in walking range of Surveyor 3

Surveyor had a scoop to dig up soil samples

??? Was Surveyor in a good state?

It seemed so, though the LM's landing blast had blown away much of the lunar dust that had settled on the probe's surfaces.

Later analysis suggested (but did not prove) that some stray Earth bacteria had survived being on the Moon over two years.

→ Surveyor's TV camera was returned to Earth for later study.

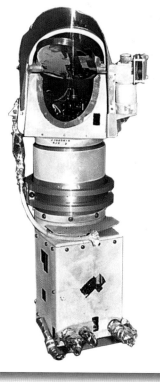

APOLLO 13
EXPLOSION IN SPACE

The third Moon-landing mission nearly ended in disaster when the crew heard "a pretty large bang."

??? What went wrong with the flight?

Apollo 13 launched on April 11, 1970. Nearly 56 hours later, Commander Jim Lovell, CM Pilot John "Jack" Swigert, and LM Pilot Fred Haise were settling in to the flight. They were about 205,000 miles (330,000 km) from Earth when suddenly an oxygen tank in the Service Module exploded.

← Fuel cells in the service module used hydrogen and oxygen to make electricity, with the waste being pure water. The exploding tank meant power and water were no longer available. This put the astronauts at great risk.

??? Did Apollo 13 carry an emergency lifeboat?

Not like a ship's lifeboat. Instead, the Lunar Module Aquarius performed the same job. The crew used it to save their lives. After the explosion, the Command Module Odyssey lost power and with it, cabin heat and the supply of drinking water. Even worse, the air supply was becoming impure and unbreathable. Essential repairs were needed urgently.

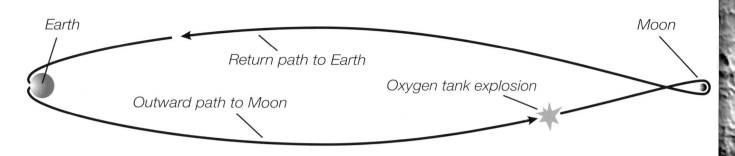

Earth

Return path to Earth

Oxygen tank explosion

Moon

Outward path to Moon

??? How did the LM Aquarius save the mission?

Aquarius was already docked to the Odyssey, ready for Lovell and Haise's Moon-landing trip. The crew managed to use the LM's power supply for heat and light. They also used the LM to help filter their oxygen.

↑ The looping flight path of Apollo 13. From launch to **splashdown**, the mission lasted 11 days.

↑ The damaged Service Module, photographed from inside the Command Module.

→ Jack Swigert (right) holds the apparatus that kept the Command Module air clean enough to breathe safely.

??? How did they breathe?

We breathe out **carbon dioxide** when we exhale, but it's poisonous if breathed in again. To clean the CM's air, the crew (with instructions from Mission Control) linked the LM and CM using a space-suit hose, the device being nicknamed "the postbox."

→ Safely back, the Apollo 13 crew stand aboard the USS Iwo Jima.

APOLLO 14
SCIENCE ON THE MOVE

A small cart was made for astronauts to carry research equipment. But there was also time for some lunar golf!

The MET was nicknamed the "lunar rickshaw"

??? Where did Apollo 14 land?

Commander Alan Shepard and LM Pilot Edgar Mitchell set down safely in an area of lunar highlands around Fra Mauro, a 50-mile-wide (80 km) crater named after an Italian mapmaker from the 1400s.

The mission had too many measuring instruments to carry them all by hand. Instead, Mitchell and Shepard used a specially designed two-wheel handcart, called the Modular Equipment Transporter (**MET**).

→ This TV image shows Alan Shepard taking a golf shot using the makeshift club (arrowed) he had taken to the Moon.

??? Was there a chance of another explosion, like Apollo 13?

Space flight is dangerous, and something might go wrong at any time. However, changes were made to the Service Module before Apollo 14 was launched. These changes included a redesigned oxygen system, including the tank that had exploded during the Apollo 13 flight.

The extra work involved meant that Apollo 14's launch was delayed four months, to January 31, 1971.

⬇ The Lunar Module Antares was the base for the Apollo 14 landing, which lasted for just over 33.5 hours.

⬆ The top layer of Moon soil is very powdery. Astronaut moon boots easily made impressions in it.

??? What were the "Moon trees"?

These were 500 seeds carried aboard the CM Kitty Hawk by the pilot, Stuart Roosa. On return to Earth, most of them germinated, proving that a journey through space had not harmed them. Many of the seeds have since grown into adult trees.

➜ This is a Moon tree grown from the seed of an original Moon tree. It was planted in England.

LUNAR ROVING VEHICLE
AN ELECTRIC CAR FOR TWO

The electric-powered Lunar Roving Vehicle (LRV) carried two astronauts and equipment, plus any rock and soil samples they collected.

??? How many LRV "Moon buggies" were made?

Three lunar rovers were built. All were designed to work in a low-gravity environment. Riding in an LRV, astronauts could explore far from their landing site.

Radio antenna

TV camera

↑ Apollo 16 astronauts ride in the Earth trainer LRV.

??? How fast could the LRV travel?

The LRV was not speedy, but could still move at 8 miles per hour (12 kph), twice the speed of a walking astronaut. The LRV above had rubber tires for test-drives on Earth. On the Moon, they were made of metal mesh.

"It was the ride of my life." Charles "Charlie" Duke, LM pilot, Apollo 16. He was then 36 years old, the youngest person to walk on the Moon, or to drive an LRV.

??? How was an LRV carried to the Moon?

The design team created a machine that folded neatly into a compartment (*1-4 sequence above*) in the LM. This had about the same volume as the back of an SUV vehicle.

→ Technicians check out the folding mechanism of an LRV, before it is made ready for flight.

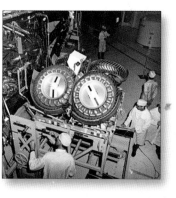

↓ The Apollo 15 LRV was included in this 1971 postage stamp, issued after the success of the mission.

US 8c

US 8c

UNITED STATES IN SPACE... A DECADE OF ACHIEVEMENT

APOLLO 15
DRIVING ON ANOTHER WORLD

A lunar rover was used on the Apollo 15 mission, allowing Commander David Scott and LM Pilot James Irwin to explore farther than previous landings had done on foot.

Hadley Rille

Landing site

??? Where was the landing zone?
The target for the July 1971 landing was the Hadley Rille area. A rille is a long channel that snakes across the surface.

↑ Apollo 15 landed next to the curving Hadley Rille.

??? How was the LRV controlled?
When unpacked from the Lunar Module's descent stage, the LRV was good to go. It had four electric motors, one in the hub of each wheel, and was steered by using a central T-shaped control stick.

↑ To steer the LRV, James Irwin used the central control stick (inset).

Moving the stick from side to side controlled the steering, pushing it forward or back made the LRV move ahead or go in reverse.

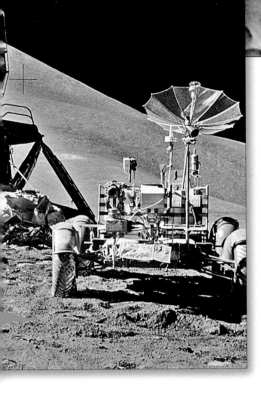

??? How much did the LRV weigh?

The design team aimed to keep weight as low as possible. Back on Earth, the empty LRV weighed 463 pounds (210 kg), but in the low lunar gravity, its weight was just 77 pounds (35 kg).

??? What happened in the CSM?

As on other Apollo missions, there was plenty for the third crew member to do in the CSM. CM Pilot Alfred Worden was in charge of measuring equipment packed into the Scientific Instrument Module (**SIM**, *arrowed above*).

Observations included photographing the surface and measuring the exact height of various features. There was also a small subsatellite which was launched from the SIM bay before they all left the Moon for the return to Earth.

> "...looked so fragile, so delicate, that if you touched it with a finger it would crumble and fall apart."
> *James Irwin, LM pilot, Apollo 15, on his view of our world hanging against the blackness of space*

Fallen Astronaut *figure*

??? What is the Fallen Astronaut?

It is a small figure made of aluminum, created by Paul van Hoeydonck, a Belgian artist.

The *Fallen Astronaut* was placed on the Moon by David Scott. It lies next to a metal plaque, marking the names of 14 dead astronauts and cosmonauts, some of whom died in spacecraft accidents.

EXPLORING THE LUNAR HIGHLANDS

Like Apollo 15 and the later 17, Apollo 16 took a Lunar Roving Vehicle, and carried enough supplies to last for a three-day stay on the Moon.

??? Where did Apollo 16 touch down?

Commander John Young and LM Pilot Charles "Charlie" Duke set down on April 21, 1972. They landed in a region called Descartes, thought to be an interesting target zone, especially as it is situated 7,400 feet (2,260 m) higher than the Sea of Tranquility, where Apollo 11 had landed in 1969.

??? What was different about the Descartes region?

Earth scientists believed it was made of rocks older than the lower lunar "seas."

Taking samples here would help researchers piece together answers to key scientific questions, such as the age of the Moon, and whether it shares a similar makeup to Earth.

← Moon dust covered the astronauts' space suits in a short time. There were three Moon walks, so Young and Duke carried lunar dust inside the LM each time they climbed back inside.

??? What was ALSEP?

The Apollo Lunar Surface Experiments
Package (**ALSEP**) was a series of research
instruments laid out by astronauts after
landing safely. Various instruments were
used, such as the seismometer (*arrowed at
right*), which could measure **moonquakes**.

Another important ALSEP device was
a reflector system, which allowed super-
accurate measurements of the distance
between Earth and the Moon.

→ Young and Duke recorded their takeoff, using the
LRV's color TV camera. Here, the ascent stage of the
LM blasts free of the descent stage. Next stop, docking
with the CSM and its pilot, Thomas "Ken" Mattingly,
waiting for them high in lunar orbit.

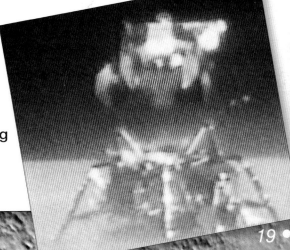

APOLLO 17
THE LAST LANDING

Apollo 17 was the sixth and final lunar-landing mission. No humans have traveled beyond Earth's orbit since that mission.

??? What was Harrison Schmitt's main aim?

Apollo 17 was the final Moon mission of the Apollo program. The LM Challenger made a safe landing in the Taurus-Littrow valley on December 11, 1972. On board were Commander Eugene Cernan and LM Pilot Harrison Schmitt.

Like previous Apollo missions, the plan was to study the area and take rock samples back to Earth. Schmitt was a geologist, so could look at the valley with a trained eye.

↑ This photo of Earth became known as the "blue marble." It was taken from the CM America on the way to the Moon.

??? What repairs did they have to make?

An unexpected problem was a broken fender on the LRV, which threw up a spray of Moon dust over the astronauts as soon as they picked up speed. They carried a roll of duct tape in the LM, and after some trial and error, managed to stick the fender in place. After this, the LRV gave them no further problems.

↑ Eugene Cernan photographed Harrison Schmitt standing next to a huge rock. Their LRV is parked on the far side.

"It's like trying to describe what you feel when you're standing on the rim of the Grand Canyon...You have to be there to really know what it's like."

Harrison Schmitt, Apollo 17 LM pilot

??? What happened to the LM?

The empty LM met its end with a crash into the Moon. Its impact was measured by various instruments on the surface.

Apollo 17 broke several records, including the most time spent on the Moon, and the biggest load of rock samples.

→ CM Pilot Ronald Evans made a spacewalk on the way home to recover exposed film from the SM.

WILL WE VISIT THE MOON AGAIN?

After Apollo 17, many people thought the next step for space exploration would be a Moon base. Few believed that no humans would return to the Moon.

??? Why did the Apollo missions come to an end?

Basically, the whole Apollo program was aimed at beating the **Soviet Union** to the Moon. And the Space Race was over the moment Neil Armstrong set foot on the Moon. After that, budget cuts meant that the original **NASA** plans for Apollo 18, 19, and 20 were canceled.

??? What happened to unused Apollo materials?

After the Moon landings, Apollo hardware was used for several other projects, including the Skylab space station, and an American-Soviet linkup in Earth orbit. But after Apollo, most U.S. effort went into creating the winged Space Shuttle, which first went into space in 1981.

Astronauts flying the Space Shuttle helped to construct the International Space Station (ISS), which continues to orbit Earth.

↑ An Apollo CSM (left) docked with the Skylab in 1973–1974.

??? What's stopped us going back to the Moon?

With human space flight, the problem has been mostly lack of money. But there have been plenty of robotic Moon missions since Apollo 17. These are cheaper to build and fly, and have carried out useful scientific research.

← The **LADEE** probe was launched by NASA in 2013. Spacecraft from China, Europe, India, Japan, and Russia have also been sent to the Moon since the Apollo missions.

"*I've always wanted to be part of something that would radically change the world…All of humanity went to the Moon with the Apollo missions. The issue was cost. There was no chance to build a base and create frequent flights. That's the problem I would like to solve.*"
Elon Musk, founder, **SpaceX**

??? Will a Moon base ever be built?

At least one person is aiming to restart Moon flights. Elon Musk, who runs the rocket company SpaceX, aims to fly there in the mid-2020s, with the Starship spacecraft.

Using the huge Starship, many old sci-fi dreams of space flight could come true at last. Starships may also fly to Mars, and perhaps go even further, to the outer planets.

↑ An artist's illustration depicts three Starship-type rockets with supplies for a growing Moon base. People live safely in domes made from crushed Moon soil.

SECRETS OF THE MOON

Six successful Apollo missions allowed a dozen astronauts to gather plenty of information about our only permanent natural **satellite**—the Moon.

↑ Buzz Aldrin stands next to a seismometer, which measures ground movements. The LLRR (circled) lies just beyond.

??? Are any Apollo instruments working?

Mostly not, but Apollo 11, 14 and 15 left a Lunar **Laser** Retro Reflector (**LLRR**). This can reflect a laser beam back to Earth, allowing scientists to measure the precise distance between Earth and the Moon.

It determined that the Moon is slowly moving away from the Earth, at 1.5 inches (3.8 cm) every year.

→ Here are the Apollo Moon-landing crews. The missions were successful, apart from Apollo 13, where an oxygen tank explosion stopped the landing attempt.

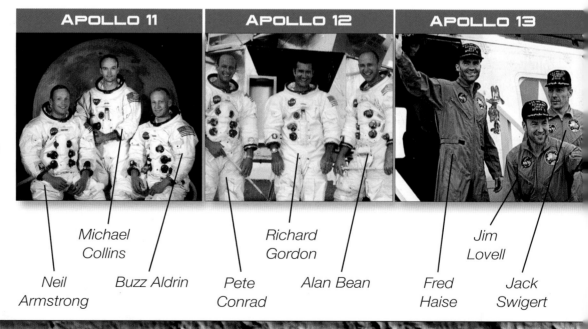

APOLLO 11	APOLLO 12	APOLLO 13

Michael Collins

Neil Armstrong

Buzz Aldrin

Richard Gordon

Pete Conrad

Alan Bean

Jim Lovell

Fred Haise

Jack Swigert

??? Did they find life on the Moon?

Before the Moon landings, plenty of people thought there might be "something" alive on the Moon, even if only some microscopic bugs.

When the first Apollo astronauts returned to Earth, they went into medical **quarantine** inside a tightly sealed trailer. They were examined for signs of alien life, but nothing at all was found, and the checks were dropped after Apollo 14.

⬆ Apollo 11 astronauts wearing quarantine suits.

??? Was walking on the Moon difficult?

Until the first robot probes landed safely, no one knew if the Moon's surface was solid or not. It might even have been buried under a deep layer of gray dust.

Buzz Aldrin's boot print (*left*) shows the reality. The Moon is easy to walk on, with a solid surface covered with loose, dusty material, called **regolith**.

⬆ *Aldrin's lunar boot print*

"I'm convinced that before the year 2000 is over, the first child will have been born on the Moon."
Optimistic prediction by Wernher von Braun, the man behind the Apollo program. It has not yet come true, but in the future, that first child may be just one of many.

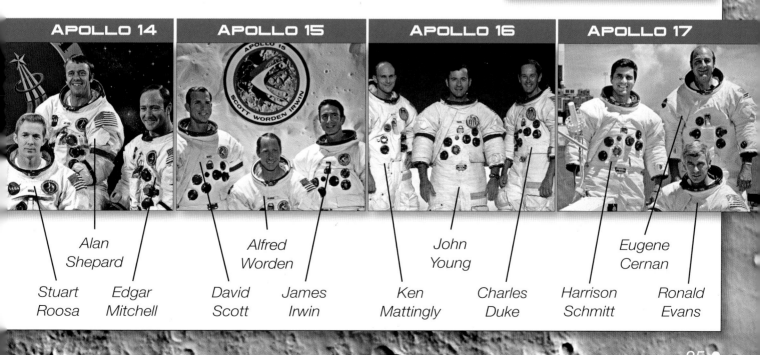

APOLLO 14	APOLLO 15	APOLLO 16	APOLLO 17

Alan Shepard

Alfred Worden

John Young

Eugene Cernan

Stuart Roosa

Edgar Mitchell

David Scott

James Irwin

Ken Mattingly

Charles Duke

Harrison Schmitt

Ronald Evans

LANDING ZONES

The Apollo missions all landed on the side of the Moon facing us.

??? Where were the landing zones?
The Apollo flights aimed to set down on the side of the Moon we see from Earth (*above*). This was necessary, because landing on the far side would have meant astronauts were cut off from radio communications with NASA controllers back on Earth.

It was also vital to land in daylight so that astronauts could see clearly, especially when making their landing approach. Each lunar day lasts for 29.5 days, which allowed the fairly short Apollo missions to remain in full sunlight for their entire landing time.

??? Could a telescope be used?
Using an Earth-based telescope to observe landings as they happened was not possible. The Moon is simply too far away.

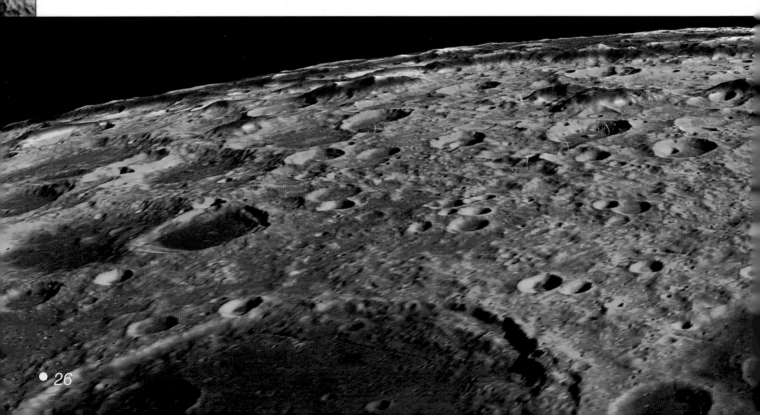

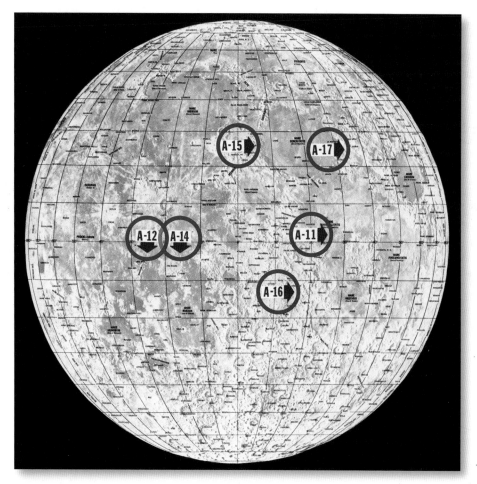

??? What about landing near the poles?

The map (*left*) shows that the six Apollo landings were all made not too far from the Moon's equator. This choice ensured full sunlight and good radio links with Earth.

Trying to land near either of the Moon's poles would have added more risks to what were already very dangerous missions.

← Apollo planners mapped out a different area for each Lunar Module to touch down.

??? Did Apollo flights land in flat or mountainous places?

The digital Moon map (*below*) shows the highest points in red and low areas in blue. Early Apollo missions went for the flatter areas. Later flights landed safely in hilly terrain.

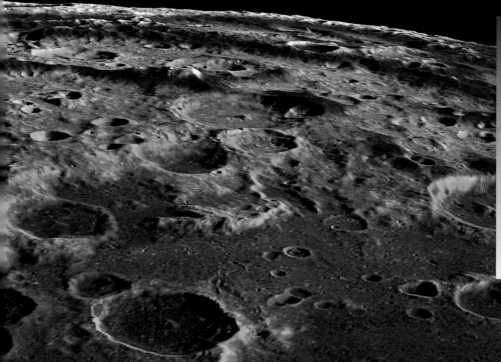

"*...I think the visual scene was described by my words on first landing— magnificent desolation. Magnificent for the achievement of being there, and desolate for the eons of lifelessness.*"
Buzz Aldin, Apollo 11 Lunar Module pilot

MOON FLIGHT FACTS/3
TIMELINE

From launch to landing, the vital statistics of six Apollo lunar landings, and one near-disaster.

Apollo 11
Launch: *July 16, 1969*
Moon landing: *July 20, 1969*
Landing site: *Sea of Tranquility*
Splashdown: *July 24, 1969*
Achievements: *First human landing on the Moon. U.S. beats Soviet Union to win the Space Race.*

Apollo 12
Launch: *November 14, 1969*
Moon landing: *November 19, 1969*
Landing site: *Ocean of Storms*
Splashdown: *November 24, 1969*
Achievements: *Precision landing. Returned parts of Surveyor 3 probe.*

Apollo 13
Launch: *April 11, 1970*
Explosion: *April 14, 1970*
No landing: *Nearest point to the Moon was 158 miles (254 km), as they looped around it for the return to Earth.*
Splashdown: *April 17, 1970*
Achievements: *Emergency work by ground control and astronauts succeeded in saving their lives.*

Apollo 14
Launch: *January 31, 1971*
Moon landing: *February 5, 1971*
Landing site: *Fra Mauro formation*

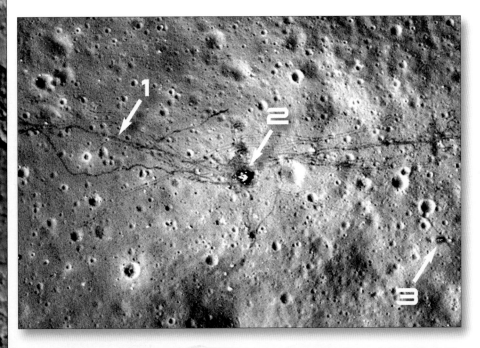

← *The Apollo 17 landing site, photographed by the Lunar Reconnaissance Orbiter (LRO) space probe, which has been at work since 2009.*

Note the tracks of astronauts (1) and the LM descent stage (2). The LRV was parked (3) to capture the takeoff with its TV camera.

Splashdown: *February 9, 1971*
Achievements: *Flew with redesigned Service Module. Equipment for the landing included the MET "lunar rickshaw."*

Apollo 15

Launch: *July 26, 1971*
Moon landing: *July 30, 1971*
Landing site: *Hadley Rille*
Splashdown: *August 7, 1971*
Achievements: *First Lunar Roving Vehicle in use. Extended three-day mission. Detailed mapping of the Moon from the orbiting Command Module.*

Apollo 16

Launch: *April 16, 1972*
Moon landing: *April 21, 1972*
Landing site: *Descartes Highlands*
Splashdown: *April 27, 1972*
Achievements: *Second LRV used for exploring the surface. Disproved theory that the area was volcanic.*

Apollo 17

Launch: *December 7, 1972*
Moon landing: *December 11, 1972*
Landing site: *Taurus-Littrow valley*
Splashdown: *December 19, 1972*
Achievements: *Third LRV taken to drive on the surface. Longest Moon landing. The most lunar samples returned to Earth. Final Apollo mission.*

After Apollo: Skylab

A U.S. space station made from a converted Saturn rocket tank. Used by U.S. astronauts

↑ *The Command Module of Apollo 15 came down with one of its three main parachutes unopened. But the system was designed for partial failure, and the crew survived unhurt.*

for about 24 weeks, from May 1973 to February 1974. An Apollo CSM was used to take crews to and from Skylab.

Apollo-Soyuz Test Project

A linkup in space in July 1975, between an Apollo CSM and a Soviet Soyuz spacecraft.

"Millions of people were inspired by the Apollo program. I was five years old when I watched Apollo 11 unfold on television, and without any doubt it was a big contributor to my passions for science, engineering, and exploration."
Jeff Bezos, founder of Amazon and the space company Blue Origin

GLOSSARY

ALSEP Apollo Lunar Surface Experiments Package. Instruments left at all Apollo landing sites, except Apollo 11 which had a simpler set.

Apollo The U.S. Moon-landing program, named after the Greek and Roman god of light and beauty

carbon dioxide Waste gas breathed out by humans and other animals. A danger in the Apollo 13 mission as it is unbreathable.

fuel cell Equipment that generates electricity by combining hydrogen and oxygen, with pure water as waste

gravity The force of attraction between objects. The Moon has six times less gravity than the Earth, so a 132-pound (60 kg) weight on Earth weighs just 22 pounds (10 kg) on the Moon.

LADEE Lunar Atmosphere and Dust Environment Explorer. A space probe that studied trace gases and dust around the Moon, from 2013 to 2014.

laser Ultra-precise beam of light

LLRR Lunar Laser Retro Reflector. An instrument left at the Apollo 11, 14, and 15 landing sites. Used to measure distances between Earth and the Moon.

LRV Lunar Roving Vehicle

MET Modular Equipment Transporter

module Section of a spacecraft that links with another. The Apollo system consisted of a number of such modules:

    CM Command Module

    CSM Command/Service Module

    SM Service Module

    LM Lunar Module

moonquake Tremors in the Moon, the lunar version of an earthquake

NASA National Air and Space

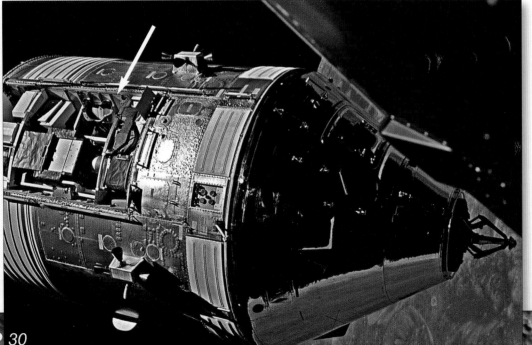

← The Apollo 17 CSM, seen from a window in the Lunar Module. SIM equipment was carried in the side (arrowed).

↑ Apollo 11 and 12 crews spent 21 days in the mobile quarantine facility, which was a specially converted Airstream trailer.

Administration, the U.S. space agency

orbit The curving path that one space object takes around another

quarantine To be kept in isolation, so stopping the spread of disease

regolith A term for Moon soil, mostly fine and powdery on top, with sand and rocks below

satellite A space object that orbits a bigger one. The Moon is Earth's natural satellite, while the CSM became an artificial satellite when it went into orbit around the Moon.

SIM Scientific Instrument Module, carried in the side of Apollo 15, 16, and 17 service modules

Soviet Union A group of 15 states, including Russia, that existed from 1922 to 1991. In the 1960s, the Soviet Union competed with the U.S. to try and win the Space Race to the Moon.

SpaceX A space company run by Elon Musk

splashdown Final part of an Apollo mission when the CM parachuted into the sea

stage Part of a rocket. Typically left behind, when empty of fuel. The descent stage of the Lunar Module acted as a landing platform, then it became a takeoff pad for the ascent stage.

WEBFINDER

There is plenty of Internet information on the Apollo program, and even more on space exploration in general. Try these sites to start with, then you can go off on your own online explorations.

www.buzzaldrin.com
Buzz Aldrin stepped onto the Moon after Neil Armstrong, but he is a leader on the Internet. Here is his fascinating personal website.

www.nasa.gov
The gold standard for space research, including thousands of pages on the Apollo program. Just use the search box to find out more.

www.canada.ca/en/space-agency
Canada's space efforts have a long history, and its robotic equipment works hard in space. Start here to find the whole story.

www.spacex.com
SpaceX plans to fly many NASA missions, now and in future. Its aims include flights to the Moon, and possibly to the planet Mars.

Was the Apollo program a fake?
It's a question that's been asked again and again, especially by people making YouTube videos. But their accusations don't stand up at all, as they mostly suggest photo or video errors, which are easily explained by experts.

Even present-day flights are called fakes by some people. How will they react to future landings? China landed a lunar rover on the far side of the Moon in January 2019. SpaceX plans Moon orbit flights in the future.

INDEX

ABOUT THE AUTHOR

David Jefferis has written many books on science and technology.

His works include a seminal series called World of the Future, as well as more than 40 science books for Crabtree Publishing.

David's merits include winning the London Times Educational Supplement Award, and also Best Science Books of the Year.

At the time of the Apollo landings, he created news graphics for the international media, and has been a keen enthusiast for space flight and high tech ever since.

Follow David online at:
www.davidjefferis.com